Strawberry and
The Sensations

Peter Viney

Garnet
Oracle

Garnet
EDUCATION

Peter Viney – author of this book, and Series Editor of the Garnet Oracle Readers – has over 40 years' experience teaching English and writing ELT materials. He now combines his writing with lecturing and teacher-training commitments internationally. He has authored and co-authored many successful textbook series and developed a wide range of highly popular video courses. Peter has been series editor and author on a number of graded reader series, and has also published with Garnet Education the highly popular *Fast Track to Reading*.

Published by
Garnet Publishing Ltd.
8 Southern Court
South Street
Reading RG1 4QS, UK

www.garneteducation.com

Copyright © Garnet Publishing Ltd 2014

The right of Peter Viney to be identified as the author of this work has been asserted in accordance with the Copyright, Design and Patents Act 1988.

ISBN 978 1 90757 528 0

First published 2014.
Reprinted 2014.

British Cataloguing-in-Publication Data
A catalogue record for this book is available from the British Library.

Production
Series editor: Peter Viney
Editorial: Clare Chandler,
                        Lucy Constable
Design and layout: Mike Hinks
Illustration: Kay Dixey

Printed and bound in Lebanon by International Press: interpress@int-press.com

Tucker International Promotions Present

STRAWBERRY AND THE SENSATIONS

CYNDI, DENISE, BOBBI
WITH THEIR BAND:

HANK MARTIN	CLIVE CARTER	BILL COLLINS	BRIAN OZ	JASON BRANFORD
GUITAR	BASS GUITAR	DRUMS	KEYBOARDS	SAXOPHONE

IN CONCERT

ARCADIA STATE CONCERT HALL
1350 South Boulevard, Greenfields, Arcadia

NOVEMBER 23rd   Two shows: 6:30 p.m. and 10:00 p.m.

1 Nobody speaks to Cyndi!

'... I just can't forget

that day we met

those days with you

the skies were blue.'

Suddenly there were no lights. Everybody stood up in the dark concert hall. They were screaming and shouting, 'More! More! More!'

'That's the end of the show, and it's "Goodnight" from *Strawberry and The Sensations*. Goodnight!' shouted Cyndi into her microphone. Then she turned and ran between the speakers to the side of the stage. She ran down the stairs to the dressing rooms. The lights went on in the concert hall, and six thousand people got up and began to move slowly towards the exits.

A road manager gave Cyndi a towel for her face. Bobbi and Denise were drinking water in the corridor outside their dressing room.

'That was a great show ... the best!' said Bobbi.

Cyndi laughed. 'Yeah, well, there's only one more show and that's the end of the concert tour for this year. What's the time?'

'Nine p.m.,' said Denise. 'We have an hour before the second show.'

'Right, I need a nice ice-cold drink,' said Cyndi.

Their band was coming off the stage. They were laughing.

'Good show, Cyndi,' said Hank. He was the guitar player.

'The singing was OK. I don't know about the very loud guitar solos!' said Cyndi. 'I couldn't hear the other guys!' Then she saw Hank's face. 'Don't worry, Hank. That was a joke.'

'Yeah, right. Very funny,' said Hank. But he was smiling.

'I'm going to get a drink, Hank,' she said. 'What do you guys want?'

'It's OK, I'm good,' said Hank. 'I still have a bottle of water from the show ...'

'Pardon me ... Ms Strawberry ... may I speak with you for a moment?'

Cyndi turned around. A police officer was standing behind her. A road manager moved in front of him, and put up his hand.

'Sorry, officer, no autographs,' he said. 'No way.'

'But I'm the police chief,' said the officer angrily.

'I said "No way". She's tired. She has another show. You can't have her autograph,' said the road manager. 'But you can have a photograph,' he gave the police officer a picture. 'There you go.'

'I don't want a photograph,' said the police chief.

'It's alright,' said Cyndi. 'No problem. He can have an autograph. Give me a pen.'

'I don't want an autograph either,' said the police chief. 'Look, Ms Strawberry, where can we speak?'

The road manager was angry. 'Nobody speaks with Cyndi between shows. Not the police chief, not the President of the United States of America. Nobody. OK?'

The police chief looked at Cyndi. 'This is important,' he said. 'This is police business. I have to speak with you, Ms Strawberry. And I must speak with you alone.'

'It's OK,' Cyndi said to the road manager. She turned to the officer. 'My name's not "Ms Strawberry". Everybody calls me "Strawberry" because of my hair. My name's Cyndi Harris.'

'Oh. I'm sorry, Ms Harris,' said the police chief. 'Perhaps we can speak in your dressing room?'

'Is it about an accident? Is my family alright?'

'It's not an accident, Ms Harris. Don't worry ..., but we need to talk.'

'OK, but I don't have much time. There's another show at ten o'clock.'

2 Stop the show!

They went into Cyndi's dressing room. She sat down and opened a small case on the table.

'Excuse me,' she said, 'but I have to do my make-up again before the second show.' She took a wet towel and started cleaning her face. 'It's OK. We can talk while I'm doing this.'

'Maybe you'd like to read this first,' said the police chief. He gave Cyndi a piece of paper.

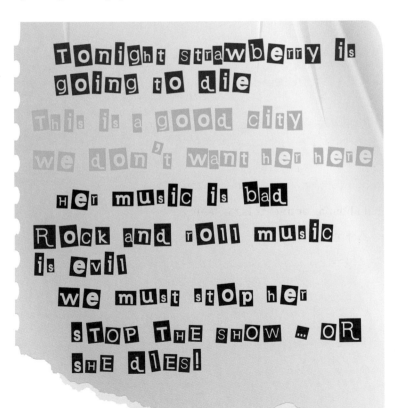

Tonight strawberry is going to die

This is a good city

we don't want her here

Her music is bad

Rock and roll music is evil

we must stop her

STOP THE SHOW ... OR SHE DIES!

Cyndi took it and read it quickly. Her face went white. 'What is this? Some kind of joke?'

'What do you think?' said the police chief.

'It's from some crazy man ...'

'Or woman,' said the police chief.

'OK, some crazy man or woman ... let's just say "some crazy guy", but you don't think it's serious ... or do you?'

'There arc a lot of weird people,' said the police chief.

'But I'm only a singer. Nobody wants to kill me.'

'Somebody does.'

'Oh, come on, be serious!' said Cyndi. 'It's just a piece of paper.'

'I am being serious,' said the police chief. 'I think we have to stop the show.'

'We can't do that! Six thousand kids have tickets. They're standing in line and coming into the concert hall right now! Arcadia's a big state. Some of them travelled for hours to the show. We flew here from Los Angeles, and it's the last show of the tour. We can't stop the show. We can't!'

'Your manager said the same thing. He also told me not to show you the paper,' said the police chief. 'But it's your life.'

'Or death,' said Cyndi. 'Sorry, that was a joke too,' she thought for a moment, 'and it wasn't funny. But nothing is going to happen. We'll be fine.'

'I don't want a murder in this city,' said the police chief.

'There isn't going to be a murder,' said Cyndi, but her hand was shaking when she took some eye make-up. She began making up her eyes.

'I have twenty police officers in the concert hall for the second show. They're going to watch you and the people at the concert.'

Cyndi stood up. 'No, we have our road managers. We don't need the police. When the kids see police all around the concert hall, they aren't going to be happy. They want to dance near the stage.'

The police chief looked at the floor for a moment, then looked at Cyndi. 'I'm sorry, Ms Harris, but nobody is going to dance near the stage. They're all going to stay in their seats.'

'The kids always dance near the stage at my shows. You can't stop them. There's going to be trouble!' she said.

'They're not going to dance near the stage, and there's not going to be trouble.' He went to the door. 'Please be careful, Ms Harris. Please be very careful.'

Bobbi and Denise came into the room. "Aren't you ready yet, Cyndi?' said Bobbi in surprise.

'Yeah ... yeah. I'm ready,' said Cyndi. 'Let's go ...'

3 Bad news

The three singers left the dressing room. Denise looked at Cyndi. 'You didn't finish your eye make-up,' she said. 'What's wrong? What did that police guy want?'

'Oh, nothing,' said Cyndi, 'nothing important.'

Brian, the keyboard player, was outside the dressing room. He was holding a newspaper. 'Look at this,' he said. He read the story to them.

Greenfield SUN November 23rd

STOP STRAWBERRY!

Four hundred people came to a meeting at Greenfield's City Hall last night.

They heard a talk about rock and roll music by State Senator Milton Bradstreet. He said, 'Rock and roll music is evil. We must stop our children listening to trash, like *Strawberry and The Sensations*.

I want the city to stop tonight's concert.' *Strawberry and The Sensations* are at #4 in the Top Twenty this week with their song 'I Can't Forget'. Senator Bradstreet doesn't like the singer because of her bright pink hair! *Strawberry and The Sensations* sold all the tickets for the show three months ago.

Bobbi took the newspaper. She laughed. 'It's a nice town!' she said.

Brian smiled. 'I asked some people here about this guy, Bradstreet. He always has some stupid story. Last month it was "No dogs in the city," and before that it was "Make people pay five thousand dollars if they drop trash in the streets." He wants to see his name in the newspaper, that's all.'

'Can I see it?' said Cyndi quietly. She took the newspaper and read the story quickly.

'What's the matter, Cyndi? You're not laughing,' said Bobbi.

'It's not funny,' said Cyndi, 'and what does he mean "evil"?' She dropped the newspaper to the floor.

'Hey! Be careful,' laughed Denise, 'or this guy will make you pay five thousand dollars!'

'Yeah, that newspaper's trash!' laughed Bobbi.

'Hey, Cyndi, smile!' said Bobbi. 'He's just a crazy guy. Don't worry about it.'

'There are a lot of people like him,' said Cyndi. 'A lot.'

The road manager came over to them. 'We're going to begin later tonight,' he said. 'The kids aren't in the hall yet. They're coming in very slowly.'

'Why?' said Denise. 'It was OK on the first show.'

'I don't know,' said the road manager. 'The police are looking at everybody's tickets very carefully.'

'What police?' said Denise. 'We never have police at our concerts. There's never any trouble.'

'There are a lot of police tonight,' said the road manager. 'They're all around the hall.'

Denise looked at Cyndi. 'So what did that police officer want? You didn't tell us.'

'Didn't I?' said Cyndi. She turned to the road manager. 'Is my microphone alright? I had a problem with my microphone in the first show.'

'What kind of problem?' said the road manager. 'I was listening to you. It was OK.'

'No, it wasn't,' said Cyndi. 'Can we go and look at it?'

'Yeah, OK. I can change it for another one. But I'm sure there's no problem,' said the road manager.

'Cyndi, what did that police officer want?' asked Denise.

'Sorry, Denise. I don't have time right now. I have to look at that microphone. I can tell you later.'

Cyndi walked away with the road manager. Denise turned to Bobbi. 'What's wrong with Cyndi?' she asked.

'I don't know,' said Bobbi. She looked down at the newspaper on the floor. 'I really don't know.'

4 Get Up and Dance

Cyndi, Bobbi and Denise were waiting at the side of the stage.
The band was beginning the first song. Hank, the guitar player,
moved to his microphone. 'Good evening, Greenfield!' he shouted.
'And here they are ... the fantastic ... the wonderful ... the
sensational ... *Strawberry and The Sensations*!'

All the kids were screaming and shouting. Cyndi, Bobbi and
Denise danced onto the stage. Cyndi took her microphone.

> *'It's a rock show, rock show, rock show*
>
> *So hold my hand and let's go, let's go, let's go ...'*

The concert hall was dark. Cyndi could see a line of police
officers in front of the stage. They weren't looking at her. They
were watching the people in the hall. The band played the first
three songs well, and Cyndi was beginning to feel better. But she
couldn't forget the piece of paper. Bobbi and Denise didn't know
about the paper, and they were standing next to her. Cyndi moved
away from them. Maybe there was a crazy person out there. The
piece of paper was about her, not Bobbi or Denise or the guys in
their band. Perhaps it was dangerous for them when Cyndi was
standing next to them.

The fourth song ended. Cyndi went over to the side of the stage,
away from the band. She went right to the front of the stage. She
spoke into her microphone.

'The next song was our biggest hit. You all know this one. It's *Get
Up and Dance.* Do you want to sing this with us?'

Six thousand people shouted, 'Yeah!'

'Do you know the words?'

'Yeah!!!'

'Do you want to ...' Cyndi stopped. She usually said 'Do you want to dance?' She looked to the side of the stage. The police chief was standing there. He was holding the piece of paper.

'I usually say "Do you want to dance?", but tonight please stay in your seats. There are a lot of people here, and the police don't want you to dance. They want everyone to stay in their seats.'

'Boo!!!'

There were a lot of shouts and boos. Everybody was booing the police. Cyndi looked down at the line of officers. The kids were throwing things at them.

'Hey!' shouted Cyndi. 'Hey! Just wait a moment! The police are wearing blue uniforms. But a lot of people here are wearing blue jeans. It's the same thing. Everyone here tonight is wearing a uniform.'

A lot of people laughed.

'They want you to stay in your seats. I want you to stay in your seats, too! When you're booing them, you're booing me. I'm asking you to stay in your seats. Alright?'

Everybody in the concert hall was shouting, 'Alright!'

'Good! But I want you to sing! Can you sing?'

'Yeah!!!'

Hank was just behind Cyndi now. 'What's happening, Cyndi?' he asked. 'What's this all about?'

'Just play the song, Hank,' she said.

5 The man in the tower

The band started *Get Up and Dance.* They always played this song for a long time. Cyndi sang the first two verses, then Jason, the saxophone player, walked to the front of the stage and began his saxophone solo. Bobbi and Denise were dancing and shaking tambourines. Cyndi usually danced between them, but she moved away to the side of the stage again. She looked up at the white lights above her. There was a lighting tower with lights and speakers on it. Then she saw him! A man was sitting at the top of the lighting tower. He was wearing a dark shirt. There was something in his hand. Cyndi could see the light on the metal. The saxophone solo finished and Bobbi and Denise started singing the third verse. Cyndi didn't sing with them. She was watching the man on the lighting tower. He was pointing something at her … it was a gun! Suddenly she threw her microphone right at him. There was a loud screaming noise from the microphone then a louder explosion. Something hit Cyndi in the face and she fell to the ground.

The band stopped playing. Some people were screaming in the concert hall. Cyndi looked up at the lighting tower. What was the explosion? Was it the gun? She was OK, but maybe he hit someone in the band or in the concert hall? Her face was wet. She put her hand to her face, then took it away and looked at her hand. It was red with blood. Her hand was shaking.

She looked back at the tower, there were police officers all over it. They had the man, and they were pulling him down from the tower. Then she looked at the floor. There were small pieces of glass all around her, and in the middle of them she could see the gun. The pieces of glass were from the light! The microphone hit the light! That was the explosion. And the man dropped the gun in surprise.

'Are you alright, Cyndi?' Jason was right beside her.

'Yeah, yeah. It's only a small cut.'

There was a towel and a bottle of water on top of Brian's keyboards. Jason got them for her. She cleaned the blood from her face.

The police chief was on the stage. He was speaking into Hank's microphone, 'I'm sorry everybody. That is the end of the show. Someone tried to kill Strawberry ... I mean Ms Harris ... and we want everybody to leave quietly ...'

But Cyndi already had Jason's microphone in her hand. 'It's alright,' she said. 'Nobody's dead. I'm fine. We're going to finish the show!'

Bill, the drummer, started playing his drums quietly behind her. The others in the band stood there, they were looking at her.

'Alright, Hank,' shouted Cyndi. 'What are you waiting for?'

Hank began playing *Get Up and Dance* again. Then the keyboards and bass guitar were playing too.

'And it's OK! You can dance now!' shouted Cyndi.

The police chief looked at her, smiled and walked off the stage.

6 A new fan

Cyndi ran from the stage an hour later, after the last song. Six thousand kids were still shouting for more. The police chief was standing there.

'That was fantastic, Ms Harris. And you did the right thing. But how did you hit that light? It was more than twenty yards away!'

'Um, I didn't throw the microphone at the light,' said Cyndi. 'I threw it at the man. I missed!'

An older man in a white suit was standing next to the police chief. He had white hair and a red face. He walked over. 'Ms Harris?'

'Yes,' she said.

'My name is Senator Bradstreet. Maybe you read about me in the newspaper. I am so very, very sorry. I never thought that somebody ...'

'Right. But there are a lot of crazy people out there.'

'Yes. I came here when I heard the news. I really am sorry.'

'Forget it,' said Cyndi. 'Everybody's OK.'

Bill, the drummer, took Bradstreet's arm. 'Hey, you! No autographs. Cyndi never signs autographs after a show.'

'What? But I'm not looking for an autograph! I'm Senator ...'

'I'm not interested in your name,' said Bill. 'Outside! Go on, before I throw you out!'

Cyndi walked towards her dressing room. 'Excuse me,' she said to the police chief. 'I'm going to wash my face. We can talk in my dressing room.'

They went into the dressing room. Cyndi sat down. 'So, who was the guy in the tower?'

'He was a fan. A crazy one. He wrote fan letters to you and sent them to your managers and there were no answers.'

'They get thousands of letters.'

'I know. And he's not from Greenfield. He followed you from Los Angeles. He came to every show on the tour.'

'Phew!' said Cyndi. 'That's a weird thought. So why tonight?'

'This is the really weird bit. He wanted to see all the shows on the tour first, then kill you. He loves the music and didn't want to miss any shows.'

'That's a weirder thought! Why did he write about *This is a good city* and *We don't want her here* and *Stop the show?*'

'He read the story in the newspaper this morning. He wanted us to think it was someone from Greenfield.'

'Weirder again.'

'Thank you for finishing the show,' said the police chief. 'I thought there was going to be trouble.'

'The show must go on,' said Cyndi. 'Singers always say that, you know.'

'Er … you don't give autographs after a show?' said the police chief. 'Never?'

'Well, not usually. Why?'

'I'd like one.'

Cyndi laughed. 'Here's our new CD. I can autograph that for you.'

The police chief took the CD. 'I'm not a rock music fan, Ms Harris. But thank you. I'm going to keep this and remember this evening!'

Glossary

These extra words are not in the 750 words for Level 2.

autograph when somebody famous writes their name for another person

band a group of musicians

boo a shout from people who don't like a show and make the sound Booooo!

concert hall a big building where you go to hear music

dressing room a room in a concert hall or theatre; the musicians or actors change their clothes there

drop let something fall

drummer a person who plays the drums

drums see picture

evil very bad; the strongest word for bad

explosion the sudden, very loud noise and movement that happens when something like a bomb or gas explodes

glass a hard material that you can see through: *Windows are made of glass*

guitar, bass guitar see picture

guy a person; thirty years ago it usually meant a man, but in the USA now it can mean men or women

joke something that makes you laugh

keyboard see picture

lighting tower a tall metal construction for lights in a concert hall (see picture)

make-up something people (usually women, but also male actors) put on their faces; cosmetics

microphone see picture

murder when someone is killed, but not by mistake

No way! a very strong and informal way of saying *no*

police chief the most important police officer in a city

road manager someone who helps a rock group; they drive trucks, move speakers, etc.

saxophone see picture

senator an important politician in the USA, in national or state government

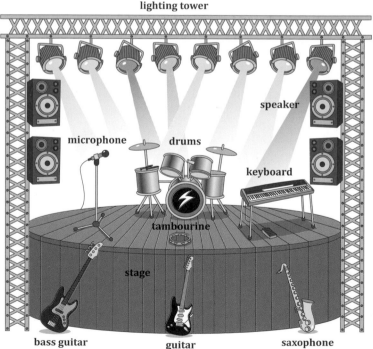

lighting tower

speaker

microphone   drums

keyboard

tambourine

stage

bass guitar   guitar   saxophone

serious not funny; important; real

shake move something quickly a short distance from side to side or up and down: *He was afraid and his hands were shaking*

solo when a musician plays alone; also when a musician is playing the loudest thing in the middle of a song

song something you can sing

speaker see picture

stage the higher place where musicians stand in a concert hall, or where actors stand in a theatre (see picture)

state there are fifty states in the USA: *Texas is a state* (Arcadia isn't a real place)

tambourine see picture

tour rock bands go on tours; they play in a different city every night

towel a piece of cotton cloth in a bathroom; you use it to make your hands, body or face dry

trash something you throw away; you have trash on a computer too

verse a section of a song: *A song has three, or four or more verses*

weird very strange and also frightening

Activities

1 **Look at the story again and find this information. How fast can you find it?**

　1　The times of the two shows.

　2　The date of the show.

　3　The number of people in the concert hall.

　4　The number of police officers in the second show.

　5　The title of the song that is #4 in the Top Twenty.

　6　The full name of the senator.

　7　The title of the song Strawberry had to sing twice.

　8　The drummer's first name.

　9　The name of the state they are in.

2 **Are these sentences true (✓) or false (✗)? Correct the false ones.**

　1　☐　It was the last day of the tour.

　2　☐　*Strawberry and The Sensations* are from New York.

　3　☐　Cyndi told Bobbi about the piece of paper.

　4　☐　There really was a problem with Cyndi's microphone in the first show.

　5　☐　A piece of glass from a light cut Cyndi's hand.

　6　☐　After the explosion, Hank gave Cyndi a towel.

　7　☐　Senator Bradstreet tried to kill Cyndi.

8 ☐ Senator Bradstreet wanted Cyndi's autograph.

9 ☐ Cyndi usually gives people autographs after a concert.

10 ☐ The police chief likes rock music.

3 Complete the sentences with words from the glossary.

1 There were lights and _____ on the lighting tower.

2 Senator Bradstreet said 'Rock music is _____.'

3 Cyndi took the police chief to the _____ room.

4 Cyndi cleaned her face with a _____.

5 Bill plays the _____ in the band.

6 The _____ when the microphone hit the light was very loud.

7 The man in the tower _____ the gun in surprise.

8 Bobbi and Denise sang the third _____ of the song without Cyndi.

9 Jason was playing a saxophone _____ when Cyndi saw the man.

10 Hank plays _____ in the band.

4 Do these comprehension tasks.

1 What were Bobbi and Denise drinking after the first show?

2 Why was the police chief angry with the road manager?

3 Why do people call Cyndi 'Strawberry'?

4 Cyndi opened a small case on the table, what was in it?

5   Did Cyndi believe the piece of paper?

6   Why didn't her manager want Cyndi to see the piece of paper?

7   Where do the kids usually dance at her concerts?

8   Why didn't Cyndi tell the others about the piece of paper?

9   Why did the second show begin late?

10   Was there really a problem with Cyndi's microphone?

11   Why did she say there was a problem?

12   Why were the kids booing the police?

13   Where was the man with the gun?

14   What did Cyndi do when she saw him?

15   What happened?

16   What did the police do?

17   Why did Cyndi have a cut on her face?

18   Why did Senator Bradstreet come to say 'I'm sorry'?

19   Who wanted Cyndi's autograph at the end?

20   Why?

5   **Search for a band on the Internet in English. Find the names of the people and the musical instruments they play. Find the names of their hit records.**

_____

_____

_____

6   Imagine you were one of the kids at the concert. You're talking to a newspaper reporter. Describe what happened and what you saw.

7 Find the words below in the word square.

autograph	serious
band	show
explosion	song
joke ✓	stage
microphone	strawberry
murder	tour

H	P	A	R	G	O	T	U	A	X
T	P	V	N	F	T	O	U	R	G
C	O	O	S	T	A	G	E	Z	B
Y	S	X	S	U	O	I	R	E	S
M	I	C	R	O	P	H	O	N	E
E	X	P	L	O	S	I	O	N	P
D	S	H	O	W	H	J	O	K	E
S	T	R	A	W	B	E	R	R	Y
Y	Z	U	B	A	N	D	A	Q	C
O	T	J	M	U	R	D	E	R	N

8 **Read the notes and highlight words which are the same, or nearly the same in your language.**

HOME SHOP CART SEARCH HELP YOUR ACCOUNT CHECKOUT

GREATEST HITS – LIVE ON STAGE!
Strawberry & The Sensations
Live at the City Theatre, Newbrook
15 July 2013

ALBUM DOWNLOAD: $8.99   **BUY NOW**
Tracks:

01	Rock Show	download NOW	99 cents
02	Jet Flight to Chicago	download NOW	99 cents
03	Valentine Card	download NOW	99 cents
04	Midnight in Mexico	download NOW	99 cents
05	Football Star	download NOW	99 cents
06	(Give Me) Rhythm ...	download NOW	99 cents
07	Princess For A Day	download NOW	99 cents
08	Boys On The Bus	download NOW	99 cents
09	Typhoon Blues	download NOW	99 cents
10	Blue Jean Baby	download NOW	99 cents
11	Get Up and Dance	download NOW	99 cents
12	Summer Skies of Blue ...	download NOW	99 cents

CD ALBUM: $11.99
VINYL ALBUM: $15.99
DVD: $15.99
Blu-ray: $22.99

REVIEW:
Strawberry and The Sensations were recorded on their North American concert tour in 2013. The tour visited thirty-two cities in fifteen U.S. states and five Canadian provinces. Includes five Top Twenty hit songs. The concert in Newbrook was broadcast live on the HBO Television Network, and streamed on the Internet via the *Strawberry and The Sensations* website. Available as audio or video files.

Other titles available in the series

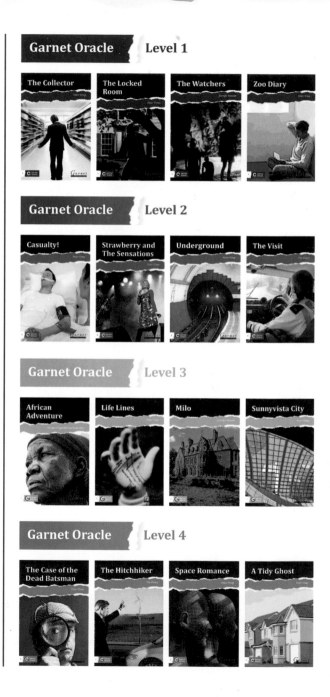

Garnet Oracle Level 1

The Collector
The Locked Room
The Watchers
Zoo Diary

Garnet Oracle Level 2

Casualty!
Strawberry and The Sensations
Underground
The Visit

Garnet Oracle Level 3

African Adventure
Life Lines
Milo
Sunnyvista City

Garnet Oracle Level 4

The Case of the Dead Batsman
The Hitchhiker
Space Romance
A Tidy Ghost